# FIERY APPETIZERS

by Dave DeWitt and Nancy Gerlach
*The Fiery Cuisines*
*Just North of the Border*
*The Whole Chile Pepper Book*

by Nancy Gerlach
*Foods of the Maya: A Taste of the Yucatan*

by Dave DeWitt
*Hot Spots*
*Callaloo, Calypso & Carnival: The Cuisines of Trinidad & Tobago*
MELTDOWN  *The Official Fiery Food Show Cookbook and Chilehead Resource Guide*

# FIERY APPETIZERS

Seventy Spicy Hot Hors D'Oeuvres
by
Dave DeWitt and Nancy Gerlach

*Illustrations by Cyd Riley*

The Crossing Press, Freedom CA

Design by Mina Greenstein

Third Printing, 1995


Library of Congress Cataloging in Publication Data

DeWitt, Dave.
      Fiery appetizers.
          p.  cm.
        1. Cookery (Appetizers)  2. Spices.  I. Gerlach,
      Nancy.  II. Title.
     ISBN 0-89594-785-4 (paper)
    TX740.F52  1995
    641.8'12--dc20               95-65
                                 CIP

# Contents

# FIERY APPETIZERS

# Incendiary Introduction

Rejoice! Cooks who love chile peppers and other fiery foods are no longer second-class citizens, scorned for eating burning dishes that terrorize the tongue, not to mention other organs. These days they're esteemed epicures who enjoy the envy of friends for serving delicious, exciting, healthy meals.

Americans consume over 560 *million* pounds of domestically grown chile peppers each year. Then there are the imports, like Mexican chiles, hot paprika, curry powder, and bottled sauces. According to our editor, it seems that every other new restaurant opening in Manhattan features fiery foods. The popularity of Mexican food alone has increased fivefold in the last decade; the epicurean status of Mexican and other fiery cuisines is now, after nearly five centuries in obscurity, finally established.

In *The Fiery Cuisines* (St. Martin's Press, 1984) we celebrated the role of chiles in international cookery, and ways of combining them with black pepper, horseradish, ginger, and mustard to create dishes both fiery and flavorful. Thousands of cooks were delighted with the idea of still more spicy food options, but a few indicated that some of their guests could not handle an entire meal of incendiary courses.

"How 'bout a book of hot appetizers?" suggested one of our friends. "That way we can seduce them gradually. Besides, a book like that could add yet another burning course to *my* meals."

The authors, never too proud to steal a good idea, especially if it involved chile peppers, immediately began a search of our vast "fiery cuisines" data base.

We weren't surprised to find that we had collected, tested, and adapted dozens of delectable appetizer recipes from all over the world, but we were astonished at the amount of anecdotal information we uncovered. Chiles aboard the space shuttle. The amazing fecundity of the mustard plant. Red pepper threatening black for spice supremacy. Emasculated jalapeños. Peppers and vampirism. The shocking spread of pungency-addiction syndrome (PAS). And much more. (Our publisher agreed that we needed more converts to the cult of chile, but balked at our suggestion to finance a world tour to test authentic recipes.)

The appetizers and anecdotes are authentic. We did invent the term "PAS," but someone had to do it. The heat scale is the one used in *The Fiery Cuisines*, with a rating from 1 to 10 for each recipe, 10 being a theoretical achievement reserved for capsaicin so powerful it can peel the paint off your Pontiac. But a chancy concoction called The Hottest Cold Plate (page 8), which is actually served during public pepper-worship ceremonies in the Sunbelt, reaches a new record: *9.2* on the heat scale.

So enjoy, but be careful. Pungency addiction syndrome is not a laughing matter. In fact, it's often tearful and can cause hiccups.

The various incendiary ingredients required for the Fiery Appetizers are increasingly available at specialty food stores and international markets. An excellent mail order source for chile peppers, hot sauces, and spices is Old Southwest Trading Company, P.O. Box 7545, Albuquerque, NM 87194, (505) 836-0168.

*NOTE:* Because of the fiery nature of chile pods and powder, it is a good idea to wear gloves while handling chiles. When transferred to the eyes or other sensitive body areas, capsiacin can cause severe burning. If you should accidentally be burned by chiles, immediately flush the eyes with water and wash other areas with large amounts of soapy water.

---

### *A Few Things Not to Touch After Handling Chiles*

| | |
|---|---|
| Babies | Eyelids |
| Cats | Genitalia |
| Contact lenses | |

# 1 · Raw Firepower

We believe in beginning with the basics: It's said that the iron-stomached cowboys of West Texas eat chile pequins, one of the hottest chile peppers in the world, right off the bush. If they can do it, so can you.

There's little or no cooking needed for these selections—they already have all the heat they need. The sauces can be used by themselves or in combination with other recipes. Picante Sauce (page 6) is our version of Tabasco and other bottled sauces like hot Pickapeppa from Jamaica. Sunbelt Salsa (page 7) and Tunisian Pepper Sauce (page 10) owe their origin to the American Southwest and Africa, respectively.

A great many raw vegetables can absorb pungency from the chiles and other spices here: cucumbers, onions, mushrooms, olives, cauliflower, carrots, broccoli, and even walnuts. Choose the vegetables you like best, and remember that, generally, the longer they sit, the higher the heat scale.

Beware The Hottest Cold Plate (page 8). It consists of pickled chiles so outrageously hot we recommend them only to serious chileheads.

# SCORCHING STUFFED CUCUMBERS

Once you've tried these, "cool as a cucumber" will never sound the same again.

1 large or 4 small cucumbers
Salt

CREAM CHEESE FILLING
4 green chiles, skinned, seeds removed,
    chopped fine
1 package (8 ounces) cream cheese
2 tablespoons milk or as needed
1 tablespoon minced onion
Pinch of garlic salt

Score the outside of the cucumber with a fork or zester. Cut off one end of the cucumber and scoop out the seeds. Salt the inside of the cucumber and stand the open end on paper towels to drain for 15 to 30 minutes.

Prepare the filling by combining all the ingredients and beating until creamy, adding more milk if necessary (the filling should remain somewhat firm).

Pack the filling tightly into the cucumber, wrap with plastic wrap, and refrigerate overnight.

*Yield:* 20 to 25 slices

*Serving Suggestion:* Cut crosswise into ¼-inch-thick slices and serve on crackers.

*Variations:* Make cucumber boats by cutting off both ends of the cucumbers, slicing lengthwise, and scooping out seeds. Proceed as above.

*Note:* This recipe requires advance preparation.

HEAT SCALE: 4

# PICANTE SAUCE

One of the all-time highs on the heat scale, this sauce should be used with caution.

½ cup vinegar
24 dried cayenne, santaka, or pequin chile peppers
1 small onion, chopped
1 teaspoon salt

Boil the vinegar and pour it over the other ingredients in a Pyrex Ball jar or sealable Pyrex canning jar. Seal and let sit for 2 weeks.

Puree the mixture and store in small bottles.

*Yield:* ½ cup

*Serving Suggestion:* Use Picante Sauce to add intense heat to other recipes or to any food considered bland.

*Note:* This recipe requires advance preparation.

HEAT SCALE: 9

---

*Debate Rages Over Pungency Addiction*

Consistent references in popular and medical literature to chile pepper "addiction," "dependency," and "uncontrolled use" have spawned a nouveau-medic-speak term dubbed "PAS"—pungency addiction syndrome. Although no researcher has taken credit for the appellation, journalists all over the world have made the condition a household word. Critics claim the term is a sensationalistic excuse for burned-out taste buds and crater stomach.

# SUNBELT SALSA

Variations on this tasty sauce abound from the American Southwest to the tip of South America. Substitute jalapeños for green chiles for a hotter sauce.

6 green chiles, skinned, seeds removed, chopped
4 medium tomatoes, chopped fine
2 cloves garlic, minced
¼ cup vegetable oil
¼ cup lime juice or vinegar
¼ cup minced fresh cilantro or ¾ teaspoon ground cumin

Mix all ingredients together in a bowl and refrigerate for at least 2 hours before serving.

*Yield:* 1½ cups

*Serving Suggestions:* As an accompaniment to meat, chicken, or fish appetizers, or with chips.

*Note:* Can be prepared in advance; keeps for a week in the refrigerator.

HEAT SCALE: 5

---

### Be Thankful They Don't Like Salsa

Dr. Roy Nakayama, the famed agronomist from New Mexico State University who developed most of the modern chile strains, once remarked on a most difficult aspect of chile gardening: "The tomato worms don't break the plants down, but the skunks come in to get the big worms and they put their little feet up on the plants."

# THE HOTTEST COLD PLATE *(Peppers en Escabeche)*

Be sure to warn guests about the high heat-scale rating for this recipe. The pickling liquid can be used to add fire to other recipes calling for vinegar or marinade.

2 *large onions, sliced into rings*
4 *cloves garlic, minced*
4 *tablespoons vegetable oil*
1 *cup white vinegar*
½ *cup water*
2 *teaspoons dried oregano*
2 *teaspoons salt*
10 *jalapeño chiles, whole, stems removed*
10 *serrano chiles, whole, stems removed*
10 *Hungarian or yellow hot chiles, stems removed*

Combine all ingredients in a covered jar and marinate for 4 to 6 weeks.

For a quicker recipe, sauté the onion and garlic in the oil until soft. Add the vinegar, water, oregano, and salt and bring to a boil. Add the chiles and simmer for 10 minutes. Then marinate the combination for 2 weeks in a covered jar.

*Yield:* 1 quart

*Serving Suggestions:* Arrange on a platter with a tomato rose in the center. Sprinkle with chopped cilantro or parsley as a garnish.

*Note:* This recipe requires advance preparation.

HEAT SCALE: 9.2—a new record!

---

### Sauces—Liquid Profits

Not counting restaurant revenues, Mexican food is now a $350-million-a-year business. Thirty percent of that is in bottled and canned sauces alone. About sixty American sauces—Tabasco, jalapeño, and New Mexico–based, are fighting each other, along with excellent imports from Mexico and Jamaica, and not to mention chile oils from the Orient.

# CAPSICUM MUSHROOM CAPS

Serve these along with the recipes in Chapter 2, Dangerous Dips, that call for raw vegetables.

1 tablespoon crushed santaka or pequin
   chiles
1 pound mushroom caps (stems removed)
1 cup cider vinegar
2 cloves garlic, minced
4 green onions, chopped (including
   greens)
3 whole cloves
½ cup olive oil

Cover the mushroom caps with the vinegar and set aside for 1 hour. Then drain the mushroom caps and place them in a jar.

Combine the chiles, garlic, onions, and cloves and mix with the mushroom caps.

Cover with the oil, close the jar, and marinate in the refrigerator for 2 days. Drain before serving.

*Yield:*   1 pound
*Note:*   This recipe requires advance preparation. It will keep in the refrigerator for several weeks.

HEAT SCALE:   5

---

### A Biting Commentary on Capsaicin, the Power Chemical

"The pungent principle of peppers, capsaicin, is a phenolic compound related to vanillin in structure. It is quite stable, persisting in apparently unreduced potency in pepper pods for considerable periods of time. It is extremely potent, and the pure form . . . can be detected by taste in a dilution of one part in one million."—Charles Heiser and Paul Smith, in *Economic Botany*

# TUNISIAN PEPPER SAUCE

The next time you broil chicken on a charcoal grill, serve this sauce as an accompaniment.

*1 tablespoon crushed red chile (or san-
    takas for more heat)*
*4 medium tomatoes, chopped fine*
*¼ cup chopped green onions (including
    greens)*
*¼ cup chopped fresh parsley*
*¼ cup olive oil*
*½ teaspoon ground coriander*
*¼ teaspoon sugar*

Combine all the ingredients in a bowl and refrigerate for at least an hour before serving.

*Yield:*   1½ to 2 cups

*Serving Suggestions:*   An accompaniment to meat, fowl, or sea-food appetizers, or as a dip for chips.

*Note:*   Can be prepared ahead of time; keeps for a week in the refrigerator.

HEAT SCALE:   4

---

*Try This When the Party Gets Dull*

The tale is told that island people in the West Indies test the pungency of bottled chile sauces by sprinkling a drop on the tablecloth. If there is no hole in the tablecloth, the sauce is rejected as too mild.

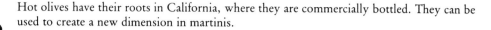

# CHILE AND WINE-MARINATED OLIVES

Hot olives have their roots in California, where they are commercially bottled. They can be used to create a new dimension in martinis.

*2 santaka chiles, crumbled*
*1 jar (14 ounces) large, pitted green Span-*
*ish olives*
*2 cloves garlic, minced*
*¼ teaspoon crushed dried thyme*
*1 cup water*
*1 cup dry sherry or white wine*
*¼ cup olive oil, or to cover*

Combine the ingredients in a jar with enough olive oil to cover them.

Cover the jar tightly and refrigerate for at least a week, occasionally opening the jar and stirring the ingredients. Drain before serving.

*Yield:*   About 1 pound

*Serving Suggestion:*   Serve the olives in a shallow bowl, speared with cocktail picks.

*Note:*   This recipe requires advance preparation. Olives will keep for about a month in the refrigerator.

HEAT SCALE:   4

---

### The Ever-Expanding Chile Belt

After Christopher Columbus returned to Europe with the first chile (erroneously called "pepper") seeds, other Portuguese traders introduced the hot fruits into the Middle East, Africa, and Asia. In fact, this hemisphere "species transfer" expanded the "chile belt," that region between about 40 degrees north latitude and 25 degrees south latitude, worldwide, where the vast majority of chile peppers are grown and consumed.

# COCONUT-PEPPER SAUCE

Especially good with seafood, this sauce originated in Polynesia.

2 tablespoons crushed red chile
1 cup shredded coconut (fresh preferred)
1 medium onion, chopped fine
⅓ cup lime or lemon juice

Combine all the ingredients in a blender and puree until smooth. Let sit 1 hour at room temperature before serving.

*Yield:* 1 cup

*Serving Suggestions:* Use as a sauce accompaniment to shrimp, fish, or chicken appetizers.

*Note:* Can be prepared ahead of time; keeps for 2 to 3 days in the refrigerator.

HEAT SCALE: 4

---

*A Veritable Rainbow of Tongue Torturers*

"The colorful reds, purples, greens, yellows, and oranges of peppers are as stimulating to our visual senses as the pungency of capsaicin is to our sense of pain."—Jean Andrews, in *Peppers, the Cultivated Capsicums,* by far the best book ever published on the history and cultivation of chile peppers.

# PICKLED POWER VEGETABLES

Don't limit yourself to these vegetables . . . onions, shallots, sweet peppers, cucumbers, and mushrooms are also delicious this way.

*Raw cauliflower, broken into flowerets*
*Raw carrots, cut into sticks or coins*
*Raw broccoli, broken into flowerets*
*5 jalapeño chiles for each 8-ounce canning jar*
*1 garlic clove for each canning jar*
*Vinegar*
*Water*
*Salt*

Pack any combination of the vegetables in sterilized Pyrex jars with jalapeños and 1 garlic clove per jar.

Prepare the pickling mixture by mixing half vinegar and half water with a teaspoon of salt for each pint jar of vegetables. Bring to a boil and immediately pour over the vegetables until they are covered. Seal the jars and allow to cool. Pickling will take approximately 2 weeks.

*Serving Suggestion:*   Serve as a relish.

HEAT SCALE:   8

# SLICED CUCUMBERS CALIENTE

Hot and slightly sweet, these Szechuan pickles complement grilled red beef.

*Salt*
*2 large cucumbers, cut into ½-inch*
*   lengthwise strips*
*2 tablespoons crushed red chile*
*¼ cup sesame oil*
*¼ cup vinegar*
*¼ cup sugar*

Salt the cucumber slices and let sit for 2 hours. Drain any excess water from the cucumber slices and place them in a nonmetallic bowl. Sprinkle the chile over the slices.

Heat the oil, vinegar, and sugar until the sugar dissolves. Pour the mixture over the slices and refrigerate for 4 hours. Drain before serving.

*Serves:*  4

*Serving Suggestion:*  Arrange on a platter with carrot curls and ripe cherry tomatoes as a garnish.

*Note:*  The slices can be stored in the refrigerator for 2 to 3 days if not drained prior to storage. Potency will be increased slightly.

HEAT SCALE:  6

---

*Peppers Give Us the Hots, Warns Priest*

"Chilli . . . if they take too much, hath bad effects, for itself is very hote, fuming, and pierceth greatly, so as the use thereof is prejudiciall to the health of young folkes, chiefely to the soule, for it provokes to lust."— Father José de Acosta, 1590.

# MEXICAN HOT NUTS

Chopped finely, these nuts can be mixed with stuffing for roasted poultry.

4 cups walnut, pecan, or cashew halves or
   peanuts
¼ cup butter, melted
2 tablespoons crushed red chile
½ teaspoon ground cumin

Combine the nuts and the melted butter and toss until the nuts are evenly coated. Spread in a baking pan and bake for 15 minutes in a 350° F oven.

Mix the chile and cumin together in a bowl. Add the nuts and stir well to coat.

Return the nuts to the baking pan and bake for another 10 minutes. Drain on paper towels before serving.

*Yield:* 4 cups

*Note:* The nuts will keep for 2 to 3 weeks, refrigerated.

HEAT SCALE: 4

---

*How Chile Peppers Conquered the World—A Hot History*
*Part I—Capsicum-Conqueror Contact*

Columbus "discovered" them, but the first person from Europe to chronicle the hot pepper was a Spanish *caballero*, El Capitan Gonsalo Fernandez de Oviedo, who wrote in 1513 that the chile pepper was beloved by Indians who "grow it in gardens and farms with much diligence and attention because they eat it continuously with all their food."

# PUNGENT PEPPER RINGS

This recipe doubles as a delicious spread for open-faced sandwiches.

1 teaspoon cayenne powder or crushed
   red chile
2 teaspoons paprika (Hungarian preferred)
1 tablespoon Dijon-style mustard
2 packages (8 ounces each) cream cheese
   at room temperature
1 cup grated Gruyère cheese
1/2 cup butter, at room temperature
12 slices spicy Italian salami, chopped
6 green onions, minced (including greens)
Salt to taste
3 each small sweet red and green bell
   peppers, seeds and stems removed

Combine all ingredients except the bell peppers and mix well.

Pack the mixture into the peppers firmly. Refrigerate for several hours or overnight.

*Serves:* 8 to 10

*Serving Suggestion:* Slice the peppers thinly and arrange the slices on lettuce or spinach leaves, alternating red and green slices.

HEAT SCALE: 5

---

*List of Chile Belt Countries That Grow the Most Peppers*

| | | | |
|---|---|---|---|
| India | Kenya | Nigeria | Tanzania |
| Japan | Mexico | Pakistan | U.S.A. |

# 2·Dangerous Dips

Here are seemingly innocent delicacies that are really the spicy quicksand of the Chile Belt. But it's not nice to trick your guests, so warn them in advance to sample conservatively before plunging in.

Texture is the key to dips. They must be soft enough not to break chips, yet not so runny that they drizzle off the munchie and splash on Billy Joe Bob's lizard boots. Constant practice, with the aid of Fiery Cuisines books, is required.

The presentation of dips is crucial. In the Chile Belt, cooks regularly use glass bowls, to show off their creations, or unusual containers like glazed Mexican flowerpots lined with plastic. Garnishes are getting out of hand these days, with fresh cilantro and chunks of jicama in the lead.

One famous Rio Grande favorite is included here—Chile con Queso (page 27). For best results and authentic taste, use only the best sharp Cheddar or Monterey Jack cheese—never processed or American cheese products.

# WILD GUACAMOLE

This classic Mexican salad dip is usually served bland. The addition of chiles is more authentic—and adds another dimension—fiery heat.

3 jalapeño or serrano chiles, seeds removed, chopped fine
3 ripe avocados, peeled, pitted, and mashed
1 medium onion, chopped fine
Pinch of garlic salt
Juice of 1 lemon
Salt to taste

Combine all the ingredients and mix well. Allow the guacamole to sit, covered, for 1 hour to blend the flavors.

*Yield:* 1 to 1½ cups
*Serving Suggestions:* As a dip with tortilla or corn chips and as a filling or sandwich spread.

HEAT SCALE: 4

---

*They Paint Their Peppers Piously in Cuzco*

Whoever who painted the "Last Supper" mural in the Cathedral of Cuzco, Peru, added a dish of chile peppers to the feast before Christ and His Apostles. This incident is a good example of fervent wishful thinking; chiles were unknown in the Middle East for nearly fifteen centuries after the time depicted in the painting.

# SHARP CLAM SPREAD

Guests won't clam up when they taste this shellfish-chile combination.

4 green chiles, skinned, seeds removed, chopped
1 tablespoon prepared horseradish
1 can (6½ ounces) minced clams, drained but liquid reserved
1 package (8 ounces) cream cheese
1 small onion, chopped fine
2 tablespoons finely chopped fresh parsley

Combine all the ingredients, adding enough clam juice (3 to 4 tablespoons) to make the mixture smooth. Allow to sit for at least an hour to blend the flavors.

*Yield:* 1½ cups

*Serving Suggestions:* Spread over crackers or raw vegetables such as celery and sliced carrots, or as a dip for chips.

*Note:* This dip will keep for 2 to 3 days in the refrigerator.

HEAT SCALE: 3

---

### A Pepper's Right Not to Breathe Secondhand Smoke

Writing in *Newsday,* Sylvia Carter makes an important medical-botanical observation: "Tobacco and hot peppers, as well as potatoes, belong to the same family of plants,* though tobacco cannot be planted too close to peppers, or the tobacco will transmit a virus to the peppers that will kill them. Smoking is often prohibited in pepper fields."

*Solanaceae, the deadly nightshade family—ED. NOTE.

# AVOCADO HORSERADISH DIP

A guacamole variation that depends on fresh horseradish for additional bite.

2 serrano or jalapeño chiles, chopped fine
3 tablespoons grated fresh horseradish
3 ripe avocados, peeled, pitted, chopped
1 small onion, chopped
2 tablespoons lemon juice
Salt to taste

Combine all the ingredients in a blender and purée until smooth. Allow to sit for an hour to blend the flavors.

*Yield:* 1½ to 2 cups

*Serving Suggestion:* Serve with fish, shrimp, and chicken appetizers.

HEAT SCALE: 4

---

**The Real Reason Chile Belters Love Fiery Foods**

Claude Levi-Strauss, the renowned anthropologist, believes that the chile pepper is the symbol of civilized eating among peoples of the Western Hemisphere. "It is striking, indeed, that the majority of American societies view rotted food as the prototype of precultural nourishment and consider the hot pepper, which is their principal condiment, as the element that separates nature and culture."

# CAYENNED CRABMEAT DIP

A pâtélike hors d'oeuvre dip that is particularly tasty with raw vegetables.

1 teaspoon cayenne powder
1 teaspoon Dijon-style mustard
1 package (8 ounces) cream cheese
¼ cup white wine
¼ cup grated onion
¼ cup minced fresh parsley
½ pound cooked crabmeat, flaked

Combine all ingredients except the crab and simmer over low heat until thoroughly heated. Stir in the crabmeat and serve.

*Yield:* 2 cups

*Serving Suggestion:* Serve with crackers, breads, or toast.

*Note:* Can be prepared a couple of days in advance and refrigerated.

HEAT SCALE: 4

---

*Beware of Biting Doggerel*

Pepper power is the potent power of perfectly
piquant pickled peppers to particularly
and pleasantly pixilate and
palpitate the public's palate.

—official creed of Pickle Packers International, St. Charles, Illinois

# SCALDING SALSA VERDE *(Green Sauce)*

This is an authentic Mexican sauce, excellent with enchiladas and flautas.

5 *jalapeño chiles, seeds removed, chopped fine*
1 *can (12 ounces) tomatillos, drained, chopped fine (see note)*
1 *medium onion, chopped fine*
2 *cloves garlic, minced*
¼ *cup chopped fresh cilantro*
*Salt to taste*
2 *tablespoons bacon fat or shortening*

Purée all ingredients, except the bacon fat, until smooth. Sauté the mixture in the fat for 5 to 10 minutes or until thoroughly heated.

*Yield:* 2 cups

*Serving Suggestions:* Serve with tortilla or corn chips or as an accompaniment to flautas or carnitas. May be served hot or cold.

*Note:* Tomatillos are small, green, tart tomatolike vegetables. If fresh, use 10 to 12; remove the husks and boil until tender before chopping. This sauce can be frozen for up to 6 months.

HEAT SCALE:  5

---

*So You Don't Believe the Power of Capsaicin, Huh?*

A recent study completed in Sweden on laboratory animals indicated that a dose of capsaicin soon after birth desensitized the animals' respiratory tracts, and made them less susceptible to the harmful effects of cigarette smoke and other irritants. The experiments suggest that capsaicin may become a treatment for asthma.

# PEPPERY PEANUT SAUCE

A great summer accompaniment for barbecued pork ribs.

1 tablespoon crushed red chile
2 tablespoons Coconut-Pepper Sauce
  (page 12)
⅓ cup crunchy peanut butter
2 tablespoons lemon juice
½ teaspoon soy sauce

Mix all ingredients together until well blended. Allow to sit for at least an hour to blend the flavors.

*Yield:* ½ cup

*Serving Suggestions:* Serve with raw vegetables, fruit chunks and slices, or with broiled meats or chicken.

*Note:* This sauce will keep for up to a week in the refrigerator.

HEAT SCALE: 3

---

### You Won't Find a Recipe Like That in This Cookbook

What is the worst possible chile recipe? According to Dr. Roy Nakayama, the famed chile agronomist who tasted a peculiar chile con carne at a cookoff: "Somebody used nonbrined calf's liver. It was the worst thing I've ever tasted."

# AVOCADO CHILI DIP

This versatile dip is also excellent as a dressing for spinach salad.

6 green chiles, skinned, seeds removed,
    chopped
1 package (8 ounces) cream cheese
3 ripe avocados, peeled, seeded, mashed
3 tablespoons milk
1 clove garlic, minced
3 tablespoons sour cream

Blend all ingredients together until creamy. Allow to sit for at least an hour to blend flavors.

*Yield:* 1½ to 2 cups
*Serving Suggestions:* Serve as an appetizer with chips or crackers.
*Variations:* Use as a filling for celery or stuffed pastries (Chapter 6).

HEAT SCALE: 4

---

### *The Humble Beginnings of the Chile Belt*

Chile historian Barbara Pickersgill speculates that cultivated chiles evolved from "tolerated weeds" of the Incas and Aztecs, and quotes the historian B. Cobo (1653): "Chiles hold first place, after maize, as the plant most common and of greatest esteem amongst the Indian."

# HOT ARTICHOKE-CHEESE DIP

This recipe originated in the artichoke capital of the world, Castroville, California.

1 jar (14 ounces) marinated artichoke
   hearts, drained, chopped
½ cup skinned, seeded, chopped green
   chiles   Medium
4 jalapeño chiles, seeds removed, chopped
   fine   medium
6 tablespoons mayonnaise
2 cups grated sharp Cheddar cheese

Spread the artichoke hearts on a greased shallow baking dish. Sprinkle the chiles over the artichokes and spread the mayonnaise over the entire mixture. Top with cheese and bake at 350°F for 15 minutes or until the cheese melts.

*Yield:* 2½ cups

*Serving Suggestion:* Serve hot with tortilla or corn chips.

*Note:* This dip can be made a day in advance and refrigerated before being baked. Bake as above until the cheese melts and the dip is hot.

HEAT SCALE: 3

---

### Indian Yogurt Supporters Confess Heat Defeat Breakthrough Cover-Up

A noted Manhattan Indian restaurant owner, in a copyrighted story in the prestigious *New York Times,* admitted that his people "resort to yogurt-based sauces or drinks" to smother the flames of pungency addiction syndrome (PAS). Specialists speculate that the uncovering of the yogurt connection could lead to a speedy symptomatic cure for what has been described as the "burning-yearning affliction."

# CURRY-PEPPER DIP

A versatile dip, particularly delicious with fruits such as apples, pineapples, and papayas.

¼ teaspoon cayenne powder
1 tablespoon curry powder (Madras preferred)
½ cup sour cream
3 tablespoons mayonnaise
2 cloves garlic, minced
¼ teaspoon Worcestershire sauce
Salt to taste

Combine all the ingredients and refrigerate for at least 4 hours or until the next day to blend the flavors.

*Yield:* ¾ cup

*Serving Suggestion:* Serve with cooked artichokes, raw vegetables, or fruit chunks.

HEAT SCALE: 3

---

### And They Say Gardening Is Difficult Today

A fourteenth-century friar, who will remain anonymous because of the risk of embarrassment, wrote: "Pepper ripens in the heat of the sun and serpents defend the woods where it grows; to pick it, the trees are set on fire to drive the serpents away and the pepper becomes black."

# CHILE CON QUESO

Served over tortilla chips, this sauce makes nachos, which have replaced hot dogs as the Sunbelt's favorite snack at baseball and football games.

*1 small onion, chopped*
*2 cloves garlic, minced*
*2 tablespoons bacon fat or shortening*
*6 green chiles, skinned, seeds removed, chopped*
*2 medium tomatoes, peeled and chopped*
*1 teaspoon dried mustard*
*¼ cup chopped fresh cilantro*
*2 cups Monterey Jack cheese, grated*

Sauté the onion and garlic in the bacon fat until soft. Add the chiles, tomatoes, mustard, and cilantro.

Add the cheese to the mixture and stir over low heat until the cheese has melted. Do not overheat.

*Yield:* 2½ cups
*Serving Suggestion:* Serve hot with tortilla or corn chips.
HEAT SCALE: 4

---

*Proponents of Heat Relief Push Rice*

The ever-widening debate on genuine symptomatic relief for PAS (pungency addiction syndrome) continues with a grain of truth. According to a major metropolitan daily newspaper, *The New York Times*, Michael Tong, a restauranteur from New York City, stated: "Plain white rice is the best way to cool off." Florence Lin, another grain supporter and Chinese cooking expert, declared: "Never water! Plain steamed rice is the only way!"

# CUERNAVACA SALSA

This colorful sauce is great with light-colored foods like chicken and fish.

1 large onion, chopped

3 cloves garlic, chopped

2 tablespoons vegetable oil

6 green chiles, skinned, seeds removed, chopped

4 yellow wax chiles, skinned, seeds removed, chopped, or guero chiles, seeds removed, chopped

2 large tomatoes, peeled and chopped fine

1/2 teaspoon ground cumin

1/2 teaspoon dried oregano

2 tablespoons chopped fresh cilantro (optional)

Sauté the onion and garlic in the oil until soft. Add the chiles and sauté for an additional minute.

Add the remaining ingredients, except for the cilantro, bring to a boil, and simmer for 5 minutes.

Garnish with the cilantro before serving.

*Yield:* 1½ cups

*Serving Suggestion:* Serve with Flaming Flautas (page 41), Carnitas Caliente (page 53), or as a dip with corn or tortilla chips.

HEAT SCALE: 7

---

### Residents of the Aleutians Take Note

"In these islands there are mountains where the cold winter was very severe, but the people endure it from habit, and with the meat they eat with very hot spices." —Christopher Columbus, 1493

# HEFTY HORSERADISH SAUCE

The classic sauce to serve with rare roast beef, or with fresh sliced vegetables before the main course.

*4 tablespoons grated fresh horseradish*
*1 cup sour cream*
*2 tablespoons tarragon vinegar*
*¼ teaspoon salt*

Combine all ingredients and allow to sit for an hour to blend the flavors.

*Yield:*   1 cup
*Serving Suggestion:*   Serve with meat appetizers.
*Note:*   Can be prepared in advance and refrigerated for a couple of weeks.

HEAT SCALE:   2

---

### The Highest Point in Chile Pepper Cuisine

Astronaut Bill Lenoir carried a bag of fresh jalapeño pods aboard the space shuttle Columbia in November 1982. Immediately dubbed an "astropod" by the chilehead underground, Lenoir has gained the distinction of being the first chilehead put into orbit with chile peppers.

# 3 · Simply Scorching Sandwiches and Spreads

Our lead recipe, El Pancho Greenburgitas (facing page), is hijacked (with permission) from the regionally famous Quarters restaurant in Albuquerque. Co-author DeWitt has eaten lunch at the Quarters over one thousand times since 1974. This is the payback. It's a collision-of-cultures concoction that depends, of course, on fresh New Mexico green chiles . . . but canned or frozen will substitute nicely.

Co-author Gerlach warns from experience that Pungent Poultry Pâté (page 40) doesn't work on dark rye. For some reason, highly seasoned breads conflict with these spreads. Use relatively bland breads to bring out the combination of flavor and fire in these sandwiches. Plain bagels are another collision-of-cultures solution.

Quesadillas Bravas (page 39) (translated loosely as "ferocious cheese things") are Mexican oil-fried turnovers. Flaming Flautas (page 41) are a Mexican–New Mexican amalgam of fiery "flutes."

You'll find spicy seafood combinations here, too: Startling Shrimp Spread (page 36) and Salmon Borracho Spread (page 37) provide fiery foreshadowing for Chapter 5, From Sea to Sizzling Sea.

# EL PANCHO GREENBURGITAS

A delicious collision of cultures: Eastern deli food meets Western chile cuisine.

4 portions of either lean pastrami, rare roast beef, or cooked knackwurst
2 cups grated sharp Cheddar cheese
8 whole green chiles, skinned, seeds removed
4 flour tortillas (8 inches each)

Place filling ingredients and 2 chiles on one half of each tortilla, fold over the other half and heat in a 350°F oven until warmed throughout. Slice each folded Greenburg into four sections for serving.

*Yield:* 16 portions
HEAT SCALE: 6

---

### Genetic Mutant Chile Pepper to Seduce Millions

El Paso horticulturist William Peavy, who developed the mild "Number 7103" chile, has declared: "When you're introducing people to Mexican food and it blows their head off, they tend not to come back. We wanted the perfect pepper for the untold millions who have been afraid to try Mexican food."

# POTENT PINWHEELS

Here are hot hors d'ouevres cleverly disguised as innocent canapés.

2 teaspoons crushed red chile
1 teaspoon paprika (Hungarian preferred)
½ teaspoon dry mustard
5 slices bacon, cooked and crumbled
1 cup grated sharp Cheddar cheese
1 egg, beaten
2 teaspoons butter
5 slices white or whole wheat bread,
   crusts removed

Combine all the ingredients, except the bread, to form a paste.

With a rolling pin, roll the slices of bread until very thin. Spread each slice of bread with the paste, roll up the bread, and wrap each roll in waxed paper. Refrigerate for at least an hour.

To serve, unwrap a roll and slice crosswise into 4 to 5 rounds. Place on an ungreased baking sheet and heat under the broiler for 5 minutes, or until browned.

*Yield:* 20 to 25 pinwheels
*Serving Suggestion* Serve on a platter with toothpicks.
*Note:* May be prepared ahead of time and refrigerated for a couple of days.

HEAT SCALE: 4

---

*Historians Track Origin of Pungency-Addiction Syndrome (PAS)*

The first record of chile dependency was in tropical America, where historian Alexander de Humboldt noted in 1814 that chiles "were as indispensably necessary to the natives as salt to whites."

# FIERY SHRIMP AND AVOCADO FILLING

Introduce this to your guests as "seafood guacamole."

3 teaspoons Picante Sauce (page 6)
4 ounces cream cheese
1 large avocado, peeled, seeded, chopped
2 tablespoons finely chopped onion
2 teaspoons lemon juice
4 ounces cooked shrimp, chopped
Salt to taste

Combine the sauce, cream cheese, avocado, onion, and lemon juice and blend until smooth. Stir in the chopped shrimp and allow to sit for at least an hour before serving.

*Yield:* 1½ cups

*Serving Suggestion:* Serve as a filling for sandwiches and pastries, or spread over crackers and bread. If used as an open-faced sandwich, garnish with whole shrimp, sliced ripe olives, or parsley.

HEAT SCALE: 3

---

### Let 'Em Use Pepper Sauce

Many liniments, including Cramer's Atomic Balm and Cramer's Gesic, contain capsicum, as does Nothum, a commercial product sold to prevent thumb sucking.

# CURRIED CANAPÉS

Hidden in these elegant little sandwiches is a hint of India.

*½ teaspoon cayenne powder*
*2 teaspoons curry powder (Madras pre-*
*ferred)*
*2 cups chopped, cooked chicken*
*2 tablespoons minced onion*
*½ cup chopped, toasted almonds*
*⅓ cup butter, at room temperature*
*6 slices bread, toasted on one side*
*1 cup grated Swiss cheese*
*Whole almonds, sliced mushrooms, or*
*sliced, stuffed ripe olives*

Combine the cayenne, curry powder, chicken, onion, and almonds. Add enough butter to hold the mixture together.

Cut the crusts off the toasted bread. On the untoasted side, spread the chicken mixture and top with cheese. Arrange the toast on a baking sheet and place under the broiler until the cheese melts.

Cut each slice into 4 pieces, garnish with whole almonds, sliced mushrooms, or sliced, stuffed ripe olives, and serve warm.

*Yield:* 24 canapés

*Note:* The chicken mixture, without the almonds, can be made 2 days in advance and refrigerated. Add the almonds before assembling the canapés.

HEAT SCALE: 3

---

*Why Chile Peppers Are Uncommon in Transylvanian Cuisine*

". . . the Rascians, the Serbians, although they keep rigorous fasts, are not liable to vampirism because they profusely season their food with red Turkish pepper."—The Linzbauer Codex, 1784

# CERVEZA-CHEDDAR SPREAD

Perfect before a Mexican meal of ceviche and steak Tampico.

1 pound sharp Cheddar cheese, grated
1 tablespoon cayenne powder
1 teaspoon hot dry mustard
1 tablespoon Worcestershire sauce
1 cup Mexican beer (Dos Equis, Corona, Tecate)
½ cup ripe olives, pitted and sliced

Combine the cheese, cayenne, mustard, and Worcestershire sauce. Gradually beat in the beer; stir in the olives.

Pack the mixture into crocks and refrigerate for at least 12 hours before serving.

*Yield:* 2½ to 3 cups

*Serving Suggestions:* As a spread for crackers or bread rounds, or as a filling for pastries (see Chapter 6).

*Note:* This recipe requires advance preparation. It can be refrigerated for 2 weeks.

HEAT SCALE: 4

---

### Vietnamese Dispute Rice Cure; Reveal Strange Hot Tea Miracle

"Whenever people there eat very hot foods, they drink tea, piping hot tea," claims Mrs. Bach Ngo, a chef from Hue. Quoted in a large Eastern newspaper, *The New York Times,* Ms. Ngo added: "It burns your mouth for a second, but in an instant it cools you off. It is strange, but it really works."

# STARTLING SHRIMP SPREAD

For a taste variation, try substituting crabmeat or chopped clams for the shrimp.

5 green chiles, skinned, seeds removed, chopped
1 teaspoon Dijon-style mustard
1 pound cooked shrimp
1 tablespoon white wine
1 tablespoon finely chopped onion
2 teaspoons lemon juice
¼ cup butter

Combine all the ingredients in a blender and purée until smooth. Refrigerate for at least an hour before serving.

*Yield:* 2 cups

*Serving Suggestions:* Serve on crackers or toast, with raw vegetables, or as a mold with crackers on the side (garnish with pimiento strips, chopped green onion tops or chives, or parsley sprigs).

HEAT SCALE: 4

---

### Peppers as Panacea, A to H

Below is a list of medical conditions mentioned with chile peppers that were culled from the vast chile database of popular and scientific literature maintained by the authors. These are conditions reputed to be treated or cured by chile peppers, whether by diet or other application. Only those indicated with an asterisk have any medical basis.

Acid indigestion, alcoholism, apoplexy, arteriosclerosis, *asthma, croup, boils, *bronchitis, childbirth, colic, *congestion, cramps, croup, dropsy, dysentery, ear infections, epilepsy, fever, gout, herpes.

# SALMON BORRACHO SPREAD

Don't let the innocent appearance of this spread fool you. It packs a pungent punch.

3 jalapeño chiles, seeds removed, chopped
2 tablespoons Dijon-style mustard
1 can (8 ounces) salmon, drained
¼ cup light rum
2 hard-cooked eggs, chopped
2 tablespoons lemon juice
Salt to taste

Combine all the ingredients in a blender and puree until smooth, adding more rum if necessary. Refrigerate for at least an hour before serving.

*Yield:* 1½ to 2 cups

*Serving Suggestions:* Serve on toast or crackers, or as a filling for pastries (see Chapter 6). Garnish with fresh dill, cucumber slices, or hard-cooked egg slices.

HEAT SCALE: 5

---

*List of Chile Belt Countries Excluded from This Book for Culinary, Not Political Reasons*

| | |
|---|---|
| Afghanistan | Lebanon |
| Ethiopia | South Africa |
| Iran | Uganda |
| Iraq | Vietnam |

# CHILE-CRABMEAT CANAPÉS

The butter in this recipe seals the bread and prevents a soggy sandwich.

6 green chiles, skinned, seeds removed, chopped

¼ cup Scalding Salsa Verde (page 22)

1 package (8 ounces) cream cheese

1 tablespoon lemon juice

2 tablespoons chopped green onions (including greens)

1 tablespoon Worcestershire sauce

1 clove garlic, minced

8 ounces fresh or canned crabmeat, chopped fine

1 loaf bread, slices cut into rounds

Butter for bread rounds

Parsley

Combine all the ingredients except the crabmeat, bread, butter, and parsley, and mix well. Stir in the crabmeat and refrigerate at least an hour to mix the flavors.

Spread butter on the bread rounds, then spread the crabmeat mixture on the rounds. Garnish with parsley and serve.

*Yield:* about 50 canapés

*Variation:* Serve in a bowl, as a dip, with crackers on the side.

*Note:* This spread can be frozen for up to 2 months. Thaw in the refrigerator for 24 hours before serving.

HEAT SCALE: 4

---

*American Craving Grows; Chile Deficit Looms Large*

"Although the United States raises between 88,270 and 110,683 acres of peppers of every type, yielding in the vicinity of 686,570 tons each year, the demand is such that an additional 5 to 6 tons are imported, primarily from Mexico, Spain, Portugal, North Africa, and Asia."—Jean Andrews

# QUESADILLAS BRAVAS

A *quesadilla* is a Mexican tortilla sandwich. When cut in wedges, they make a change from traditional party sandwiches.

6 *flour tortillas, 8 inches each*
2 *cups grated Monterey Jack cheese*
12 *green chiles, skinned, seeds removed,*
   *chopped*
1 *small onion, chopped fine*
1 *medium avocado, peeled, seeded,*
   *chopped (optional)*
*Vegetable oil for frying*

Wrap the tortillas in a towel or in foil and place in a warm oven to soften.

To assemble: On half of each tortilla place a layer of cheese, green chile, onion, and avocado (if desired). Moisten the edges of the tortillas with water, fold over the top, and press the moistened edges together with a fork to seal. Keep the quesadillas from drying out by covering with a damp towel until frying.

Fry the tortillas in ½ inch of oil, turning once, until golden brown. Drain on paper towels.

To serve, cut each quesadilla into 4 or 5 wedges.

*Yield:*   24 to 30 slices

*Variations:*   Any kind of spicy filling can be used. Try chorizo and cheese, refried beans and chile, chile con carne (homemade, of course).

*Note:*   Quesadillas can be prepared in advance, wrapped individually, and frozen for up to two months. To reheat, place on a baking sheet and bake at 350° F for 15 to 20 minutes.

HEAT SCALE:   5

# PUNGENT POULTRY PÂTÉ

Although the French would hardly add green chile to their pâté, perhaps they should.

6 green chiles, skinned, seeds removed, chopped
2 cups ground cooked turkey or chicken
3 hard-cooked eggs, chopped
¼ cup chopped green onions (greens included)
¼ cup chopped parsley
½ cup chopped toasted almonds
2 tablespoons Cognac
¼ cup mayonnaise, or as needed

Place all ingredients, except the mayonnaise, in a blender and puree until smooth, adding just enough mayonnaise to form a stiff paste.

Place the mixture in a bowl or a mold and refrigerate for at least an hour before serving.

*Yield:* 2½ to 3 cups

*Serving Suggestions:* Serve as a mold with crackers, on toast or bread rounds, or as a pastry filling.

*Note:* This recipe will keep for 2 days in the refrigerator.

HEAT SCALE: 4

---

*Gardeners! Chile Head Bird Raid Alert!*

Ornamental chiles, which are edible though extremely pungent, turn beautiful shades of red, yellow, purple, and orange at maturity, and are being used increasingly in outdoor plantings. However, birds are attracted by the vivid colors and are not turned off by the heat of the pods.

# FLAMING FLAUTAS (Rolled Tacos)

Flautas are Mexican "flutes," so called because of their tubular shape. These will pipe a hot tune.

1 medium onion, chopped
3 cloves garlic, minced
Vegetable oil
1 cup Scalding Salsa Verde (page 22)
1 3-pound chicken, cooked, skinned, and
  shredded
¼ cup chopped fresh cilantro or 2 teaspoons coriander seeds, crushed
  (optional)
24 corn tortillas
1 cup grated Monterey Jack cheese
Guacamole (page 18), Sunbelt Salsa
  (page 7), or Cuernavaca Salsa (page 28)

Sauté the onion and garlic in 2 tablespoons of oil until soft. Add the sauce, bring to a boil, reduce the heat, and simmer for 5 minutes.

Add the chicken and the cilantro, if desired, and cook for 15 minutes.

Heat ½ inch of oil in a frying pan until very hot (400° F). Place the tortillas, one at a time, in the oil for about 5 seconds a side to soften. (Take care not to overcook or you will have tortilla chips.) Set the oil in the pan aside, off the heat.

Place approximately 2 teaspoons of the filling and a teaspoon of the cheese on a tortilla and roll tightly. Secure both ends with toothpicks.

Reheat the oil. Fry the flautas in the oil until golden brown but not too crisp. Drain, remove the toothpicks for insurance purposes, and serve with guacamole or one of the other sauces on the side as a dip.

*Yield:* 24

*Variations:* Substitute ground chorizo and Cheddar cheese, or ground beef with crushed red chile, onion, and cheese, or your favorite taco or burrito filling.

*Note:* Flautas may be frozen for up to 2 months. To reheat, defrost and heat in a 350° F oven for 10 to 15 minutes.

HEAT SCALE: 5

# JALAPEÑO CHEESE MOLD

For an interesting variation, pour the gelatin mixture into tall, fluted champagne glasses. When unmolded, each guest will have a jalapeño-shaped volcano.

1 envelope unflavored gelatin
1 cup cold water
1 cup sour cream
½ cup mayonnaise
4 jalapeño chiles, seeds removed, chopped fine
6 green chiles, skinned, seeds removed, chopped fine
2 cups grated sharp Cheddar cheese
2 tablespoons finely chopped onion
1 tablespoon Worcestershire sauces
1 tablespoon minced fresh cilantro
¼ teaspoon salt

Sprinkle gelatin over the cold water and let sit for 5 minutes to soften. Heat the mixture over low heat, stirring constantly until the gelatin dissolves.

Combine the sour cream and mayonnaise and gradually stir into the gelatin until mixed. Then add the remaining ingredients to the mixture.

Refrigerate the mixture for 30 minutes or until slightly thickened. Stir to distribute the cheese and chile throughout the mixture. Chill an additional 4 hours or until firm.

*Yield:* 2 to 3 cups

*Serving Suggestion:* Unmold onto a platter, garnish with parsley and whole jalapeños, and serve with crackers.

*Note:* This recipe can be prepared a day in advance and actually tastes better that way.

HEAT SCALE: 6

# 4 · Fiery Morsels

It's a good bet that the first culinary use of chile peppers was in primitive marinades used to tenderize tough game like peccary and rabbit. Nothing's changed much in seven thousand years in the Chile Belt—we're still doing it with marinades for Pungent Peanut-Pork Kabobs (page 45) and Blistering Borneo Meat Kabobs (page 52). Remember that the heat increases with the amount of time the meat marinates.

Skewered meats can be served on the skewers or removed and eaten with knife and fork. If using bamboo skewers, soak them in water for at least an hour before broiling to keep them from burning. Experiment with different fruits and vegetables on the skewers in addition to the marinated meats.

A China-New Mexico collision of cultures explodes in The Wildest Won Tons (page 50), a surprising combination of won ton skins and powerful chorizo sausage. New Mexico Cherry Bombs (page 44) are so named because of their physical and taste similarities to the firecrackers.

Carnitas Caliente (page 53) is a traditional Southwest breakfast dish, often served with *huevos rancheros*, which makes a surprising—and delicious—appetizer.

# NEW MEXICO CHERRY BOMBS

The word bomb is only a slight exaggeration. For a much milder version, use cherry peppers.

24 jalapeño or serrano chiles
8 ounces Monterey Jack or Cheddar
   cheese, sliced
Flour for dredging
2 eggs, beaten
Vegetable oil for deep-fat frying

Slit each pepper, remove the seeds with a small spoon or knife and stuff the peppers with slices of cheese. If necessary, insert a toothpick to hold the peppers together.

Dip each chile in the flour, then the egg, then the flour again.

Fry in 350° F oil until golden brown. Drain and serve.

*Yield:* 24

*Variations:* Stuff the chiles with chorizo, or ground meat with cheese.

HEAT SCALE: 8

---

*Sometimes the Tongue Feels Like That After Eating Cherry Bombs*

Researchers at the University of Manitoba may have found a use for capsaicin's nerve-deadening ability. According to J. I. Nagy, a neurobiologist, high concentrations of the caustic chile chemical may treat "phantom limb pain," the apparent sensation of pain in a severed limb, which may be caused by abnormal nerve growth where the limb was cut.

---

# PUNGENT PEANUT-PORK KABOBS

This combination of red chile, peanuts, and pork is similar to many West African grilled specialties.

3 tablespoons crushed red chile
¼ cup smooth peanut butter
2 teaspoons ground coriander
2 teaspoons ground cumin
1 tablespoon lemon juice
3 tablespoons soy sauce (dark preferred)
2 pounds lean pork, cut into 1-inch cubes
1 cup peanuts, ground

Combine all the ingredients, except the pork and peanuts, in a non-metallic bowl, to make a thick sauce or paste. Marinate the pork in this mixture for at least 2 hours.

Place the pork on skewers, roll in the ground peanuts and broil over charcoal or under the broiler until browned on all sides.

*Yield:* 24 to 36 pieces

*Note:* This recipe requires advance preparation. The pork can be marinated overnight in the refrigerator.

HEAT SCALE: 4

---

*Marinate Your Own Stomach with This Authentic Reggae Recipe!*

An obscure use for chiles in the Caribbean is in *mandram*, a concoction of very hot "bird peppers," cucumbers, shallots, lime juice, and Madeira wine. A marinade for goat or pork or a nice fresh salsa for chips, you think? Nope, it's an island cure for stomach ache.

# ORIENTAL CHICKEN DRUMSTICKS

These are actually "wingsticks," which are smaller and easier to eat than true drumsticks.

2 pounds chicken wings
¼ cup ground red chile
2 tablespoons peeled and chopped fresh
   ginger
2 tablespoons brown sugar, firmly packed
4 green onions, chopped (including
   greens)
½ cup rice wine or dry sherry
2 cloves garlic, minced
½ cup soy sauce

*To make the drumsticks:*   Cut off the wing tips, remove the skin, and cut apart the two bones. Twist and remove the smaller bone. Cut the meat from one half the bone, keeping the meat in one piece. Turn the loosened meat over the attached meat to form a mock drumstick.

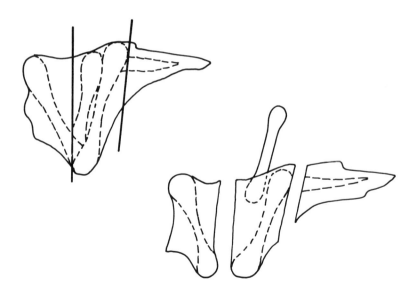

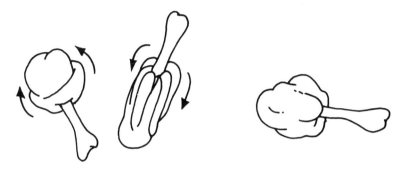

Combine all the remaining ingredients in a nonmetallic bowl and marinate the drumsticks in the mixture for at least 4 hours.

Broil the drumsticks over charcoal or under the broiler, turning and basting frequently with the marinade.

*Yield:*  8 to 10

*Note:*  This recipe requires advance preparation. The drumsticks can be marinated overnight in the refrigerator.

HEAT SCALE:  3

# CHILE CHEESE BALLS

This recipe is a hot revival of an appetizer very popular in the 1950s.

8 green chiles, skinned, seeds removed,
    chopped fine
2 teaspoons Dijon-style mustard
2 cups grated sharp Cheddar cheese
2 tablespoons finely chopped ripe olives
1 tablespoon flour
1 teaspoon Worcestershire sauce
3 egg whites
¾ cup fine dry bread crumbs
Vegetable oil for deep-fat frying

Combine the chiles, mustard, cheese, olives, flour, and Worcestershire sauce.

Beat the egg whites until stiff. Fold the egg whites into the chile mixture.

Using about a teaspoon of the mixture each time, shape into 1-inch balls. Roll the balls in the bread crumbs and chill for one hour.

Deep-fry the cheese balls in 350°F oil until golden brown. Drain and serve.

*Yield:* 20

*Note:* This recipe can be prepared in advance and refrigerated. Reheat on a rack in a 425°F oven for 5 to 8 minutes.

HEAT SCALE: 6

---

*Florida Department of Agriculture and Linus Pauling Take Note*

Given equal weights, there is about three times the amount of vitamin C in chile peppers as in oranges and lemons, six times the amount as in grapefruits, and nine times the amount as in avocados.

# FIERY FAJITAS

Once just the rage of the Sunbelt, fajitas are now being served up everywhere.

4 jalapeño peppers, seeds removed,
  chopped fine
1 cup Sunbelt Salsa (page 7)
⅓ cup soy sauce
⅓ cup red wine
2 pounds sirloin or skirt steak
8 small flour tortillas

Make a marinade out of the jalapeños, ½ cup of the salsa, the soy sauce, and wine. Trim and score the steak and marinate in the sauce for 24 hours.

Grill the steak over charcoal and mesquite until done and carve against the grain (as with London broil).

*Serves:* 6 to 8

*Serving Suggestion:* Place steak pieces on a tortilla, cover with remaining salsa, and fold the edges over to make a burrito-like sandwich.

*Variations:* Allow guests to construct their own fajitas by adding a variety of condiments: sour cream, guacamole, pinto beans. Substitute chicken or pork for the steak.

*Note:* This recipe requires advance preparation.

HEAT SCALE: 5

---

### The Only Way to Smoke Peppers

Most varieties of chile peppers can be preserved by sun-drying or other heating. But fleshy fruits like the jalapeño must be smoked much like hams are. These peppers are exposed in indirect heat and smoke in an oven, where the final result is called the "chipotle" pepper. Japaleños smoked without seeds are called *capones,* which means "castrated ones."

# THE WILDEST WON TONS

Another collision of cultures, this time Chinese–New Mexican.

6 ounces chorizo sausage or other spicy
   sausage
½ pound ground beef
1 medium onion, chopped
1 tablespoon crushed red chile
1 cup grated sharp Cheddar cheese
1 pound won ton skins
Vegetable oil for deep-fat frying

Remove the chorizo from the casings and combine with the beef and onion. Sauté the mixture until the beef turns brown. Pour off the excess fat.

Add the chile and cheese and cook only until the cheese begins to melt. Remove from the heat and cool.

*To assemble:* Place a won ton skin in your hand or on a flat surface with the point to you. Put 1 teaspoon of the mixture in the far corner. Dot the corner with water and fold over the mixture, tucking the point under the mixture. Moisten the remaining corners, bring together and overlap, pinching firmly to seal (see note).

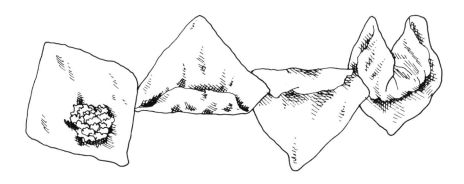

Deep-fry the won tons in 350° F. oil for 2 minutes, or until golden brown. Drain.

*Yield:* 5 to 6 dozen

*Serving Suggestion:* Serve with Avocado Chile Dip (page 24).

*Note:* At this point the won tons can be refrigerated for a couple of days, or frozen for up to 3 months. If frozen, thaw and deep-fry as above. The cooked won tons can be frozen for up to 6 months. To reheat, bake 10 to 15 minutes on a rack in a 350° F. oven, or until crisp.

HEAT SCALE: 7

---

### *Beat Me! Whip Me! Force Me to Eat the Wildest Won Tons!*

Compulsive chileheads are similar in temperament to sky divers, horror movie addicts, and others having "benignly masochistic activities," according to sociologists Rozin and Schiller. They note in a 1980 study that chile pepper lovers receive pleasure from experiencing a "constrained risk," perceived danger that is not actually forthcoming. They also found that those who liked chile peppers loved the burn despite the desensitization that occurs upon increased consumption.

# BLISTERING BORNEO MEAT KABOBS

From Indonesia comes this unusual saté featuring fruit as a part of the grill rather than as an accompaniment.

1/2 cup ground red chile
3 tablespoons curry powder (Madras preferred)
1 cup dark beer
1 tablespoon honey
2 cloves garlic, minced
1 onion, chopped fine
Juice of 2 lemons
1 pound beef or pork, cut in 1-inch cubes
Pineapple and banana chunks

Combine all the ingredients except the meat and fruit in a nonmetallic bowl. Add the meat and marinate overnight.

Alternate the meat and fruit on skewers and broil over charcoal or under the broiler until browned, basting frequently with the marinade.

*Serves:* 6 to 8

*Serving Suggestion:* Serve on individual skewers accompanied by the marinade for dipping.

*Note:* This recipe requires advance preparation.

HEAT SCALE: 7

---

### *No Wonder Chile's Popularity Is Gaining on Black Pepper*

Scientists at the Monell Chemical Senses Center in Philadelphia have discovered that not all fiery foods—they prefer the more tech-ese term "oral irritants"—assault the mouth in the same way. Chile burns the top and the sides of the tongue, while ginger attacks the back of the throat. But in an ominous development, black pepper was reported to "inhibit all tastes."

# CARNITAS CALIENTE

Carnitas are Mexican "little pieces of meat" often served at breakfast but perfect as alarming appetizers.

3 teaspoons red chile powder
¼ teaspoon freshly ground black pepper
1 teaspoon ground cumin
3 cloves garlic, minced
2 teaspoons finely chopped fresh cilantro
¾ teaspoon salt
1 pound boneless pork, trimmed and cut into 1-inch cubes

Combine all the spices and rub the pork cubes with the mixture. Let sit at room temperature for an hour.

Bake the cubes on a rack over a baking sheet for 1½ hours at 300° F, or until the meat is quite crisp. Pour off the fat as it accumulates.

*Serves:* 6

*Serving Suggestion:* Serve in a chafing dish with toothpicks accompanied by any or all of the following sauces for dipping: Wild Guacamole (page 18), Scalding Salsa Verde (page 22), Sunbelt Salsa (page 6), Cuernavaca Salsa (page 28).

*Note:* Carnitas can be prepared in advance and reheated. They can also be frozen. To reheat, thaw overnight in the refrigerator and bake in a 350°F oven for 5 to 8 minutes, or until heated.

HEAT SCALE: 3

---

*List of Chile Belt Countries for Which the Authors Could Find No Authentic Fiery Recipes. Readers' Assistance Requested.*

| | |
|---|---|
| Australia | Surinam |
| Botswana | Yemen |
| Crete | |

# CHILE RELLENO APPETIZERS

This dish is a variation of those served at feasts and weddings in New Mexican pueblos.

1 pound stew beef
1 cup chopped, skinned, seeded green
    chiles
Vegetable oil
2 cloves garlic, minced
2 teaspoons salt
2 eggs, separated
3 tablespoons flour
Flour for dredging

Boil the beef until tender, drain, and grind. Save the broth.

Sauté the chile in a little oil and combine with the beef. Add the garlic, salt, and 1½ cups broth. Simmer the mixture until thick but not dry.

Beat the egg whites until they form peaks. Combine the flour and egg yolks and thoroughly mix. Fold the egg yolk mixture into the egg whites until combined to form a batter.

Take about one teaspoon of the meat mixture, roll in flour and shape into 1-inch balls. Dip these balls into the batter and deep-fry in 350°F oil until golden. Drain on paper towels before serving.

*Yield:* 20 to 24
HEAT SCALE: 8

---

### At Last! Proof of Bizarre Chile Cult!

According to historian Garcilaso de la Vega, the Incas worshipped the chile pepper as one of the four brothers of their creation myth: Ayar Uchu (Brother Chile Pepper). "The pepper represents the delight they received from this teaching, and the word for pleasure is to show the joy and satisfaction in which they afterward lived."—*Commentarios Reales*, 1609

# TANGY CHICKEN TIDBITS

For a terrific tangy variation, skewer these tidbits, alternating the chicken with cherry tomatoes, and baste with the cayenne sauce while grilling.

3 tablespoons butter
1 tablespoon sesame oil
1 teaspoons cayenne powder
½ cup Dijon-style mustard
⅓ cup cider vinegar
2 tablespoons brown sugar, firmly packed
3 tablespoons honey
1 tablespoon soy sauce
2 pounds boneless chicken breast, skinned and cut into 1-inch cubes

Melt the butter and oil in a pan, add the remaining ingredients, except the chicken, and simmer for 5 minutes. Add the chicken and sauté until the chicken is browned on all sides, about 10 to 15 minutes.

*Yield:*  50 to 60

*Serving Suggestion:*  Serve the chicken, along with the sauce, in a chafing dish with toothpicks. Garnish with parsley.

HEAT SCALE:  4

---

### *What to Do with Chiles When You're Tired of Cooking with Them*

In most parts of the country, children who use forbidden words get their mouths washed out with soap. But in some parts of Texas, the offending children have their mouths scorched with a fresh *chiltepin*, a hot, uncultivated variety of chile pepper.

Since we've heard many reports of hot chiles being used as a fumigant for bedbugs, it's no surprise that several sources recommend sprinkling the hottest cayenne you can find around doors and windows to keep ants away.

# BURNING BRANDIED BROCHETTES

For a more colorful brochette, weave green and red pepper strips in with the chicken pieces.

2 tablespoons crushed red chile
¼ cup vegetable oil
3 tablespoons brandy
2 tablespoons honey
2 tablespoons soy sauce
2 pounds boned chicken breasts, skin removed, cut in strips
¼ cup chopped cashew nuts (optional)

Combine all the ingredients, except the chicken. Marinate the chicken strips in the mixture for at least 4 hours. Thread the chicken on skewers by pushing each skewer in and out of a chicken strip, as though sewing. Broil, over charcoal or under the broiler, basting with the marinade.

*Yield:*  24 skewers
*Serving Suggestion:*  Place the skewers on a platter and sprinkle chopped cashews on top.
*Note:*  This recipe requires advance preparation. The chicken can be marinated overnight in the refrigerator.

HEAT SCALE:  3

---

*"Okay, Give Me Three Groats' Worth—and You Deliver."*

Our wandering correspondent, Marco Polo, reports from China: "One Venetian groat will buy forty pounds of fresh ginger of excellent quality."

# BITING "BABY" RIBLETS

Of Oriental origin, this dish is simpler to serve than barbecued ribs.

2 pounds spareribs, cut crosswise into 2-inch pieces and separated into individual ribs
¼ cup cornstarch
Vegetable oil for deep-fat frying
¼ cup crushed red chile
1 tablespoon peeled and minced fresh ginger
3 cloves garlic, minced
1 tablespoon sesame oil
1 tablespoon Worcestershire sauce
2 tablespoons rice wine or dry sherry
¼ cup catsup
1 teaspoon sugar

Remove the film of skin on the back of the ribs and coat the ribs with the cornstarch. Deep-fry the ribs in 350°F oil until golden brown, then drain.

Saute the chile, ginger, and garlic in the sesame oil. Add the remaining ingredients and simmer for 5 minutes.

Add the ribs and cover with the sauce. Stir over medium heat until thoroughly heated, turning often.

*Yield:* 25 to 30 riblets

*Serving Suggestion:* Serve in a chafing dish.

*Note:* The ribs can be prepared in advance and frozen. To reheat, thaw overnight in the refrigerator and bake at 425°F for 5 minutes, or until heated.

HEAT SCALE: 5

---

*Exorcising a Fiery Ghost:* A "recipe" from the early Spanish *curanderas* (healers) of the old Southwest.

2 nails
1 piece wire 6 inches long
Hearts and seeds of 3 dried chiles
½ teaspoon rock salt
¼ cup kerosene

Tie the two nails in the shape of a cross with the wire. Place in an open fire, and when red hot, remove and set on the chiles. Sprinkle rock salt over the nails in the motion of the cross, add the kerosene, and the resultant flame will burn away all witchcraft.

# ZESTY SKEWERED CHICKEN

A version of Japanese yakitori, which means grilled meats and poultry.

¼ cup crushed red chile
1 tablespoon chopped garlic
1 cup vegetable oil
½ cup lemon juice
2 pounds boneless chicken breasts,
   skinned, cut into 1-inch cubes
1 cup small cocktail onions
Cherry tomatoes (optional)

Puree the chile, garlic, and ½ of the oil until smooth. Add the remaining oil and the lemon juice and mix well. Marinate the chicken cubes in the mixture for at least 2 hours.

Alternate chicken cubes and onions (and cherry tomatoes, if desired) on skewers and broil over charcoal or under the broiler, basting with the marinade.

*Yield:* *24 skewers*

*Note:* This recipe requires advance preparation, and the chicken can be marinated overnight in the refrigerator.

HEAT SCALE: 4

---

### Orientals Suck Lemons to Defeat Heat, Claims Surgeon

Pungency overdose, that agonizing burning sensation in the mouth and nose, combined with profuse eye tearing, could soon be a thing of the past if this Oriental secret is true. "Lemons," according to Dr. Jesse S. Manlapaz, a Philippine-born surgeon in Connecticut quoted in the respected urban daily *The New York Times*, "seem to provide relief for the lips and mouth."

# CARNE ADOBADO

Chiles and unsweetened chocolate together is a traditional Mexican combination of Aztec origin.

6 ancho or dried red chiles, or 3 tablespoons ground red chile
¼ cup chopped unsweetened chocolate
2 large tomatoes, peeled and chopped fine
½ teaspoon ground cinnamon
½ teaspoon dried oregano
4 whole cloves
1 cup water
1 pound pork loin, cut into strips ¼ inch
  thick, 2 inches long, and ½ to ¾ inches
  wide

If dried chiles are used, soak them in the water until soft and puree in a blender.

Melt the chocolate in a heavy skillet and add all the ingredients except the pork. Simmer for 10 minutes to blend all the flavors. Remove and cool.

Add the pork and marinate overnight in a nonmetallic bowl.

Thread the meat on skewers by pushing each skewer in and out of a pork strip, as if sewing. Broil over charcoal or under the broiler, basting with the sauce until done.

*Yield:* 24 skewers
*Note:* This recipe requires advance preparation.
HEAT SCALE: 5

---

## A Use Not Endorsed by the Authors

When asked what was the most bizarre culinary application of his company's hot picante sauce, Pace Food's vice-president Rod Sands replied: "I know of a man who uses it in his coffee."

# 5 · From Sea to Sizzling Sea

Shrimp is the most prevalent seafood appetizer. But frankly, we're weary of "shrimp cocktails" miserably weak in horseradish and Tabasco. So we've used ginger, red chile, cayenne, and Picante Sauce to spice them up in appetizers like Marinated Hot Shrimp (page 65) and Gingered Shrimp (page 71).

Batters provide even more shrimp variations. Sharp Coconut Shrimp (page 66) combines beer, chile, and coconut, while Piquant Pom-Pom Shrimp (page 68) uses Chinese rice noodles to puff them up powerfully.

The marinade used in Scalding Snappers en Escabeche (facing page) is the traditional Spanish-American vinegar-based sauce, which becomes a pickle if the meat being marinated is immersed too long. Pungent Pickled Salmon (page 64) utilizes a similar, but sweeter, escabeche-like marinade.

Clams Pica-Pica (page 69) is an adaptation of a delicious hot dish originally served at Los Comerciales restaurant in Cd. Juarez, Mexico. Co-author DeWitt once asked the waiter there what "pica-pica" meant. "Hot as hell," came the translation, apparently an igneous idiom.

# SCALDING SNAPPERS EN ESCABECHE

Don't let the long list of ingredients scare you off—this South American pickled fish appetizer is easy to prepare.

2 pounds red snapper fillets, cubed, or
    substitute other white fish
¼ cup olive oil
2 large onions, sliced thin and separated
    into rings
3 cloves garlic, chopped
2 carrots, sliced into coins
¼ teaspoon black peppercorns, crushed
6 whole pequin chiles, or santakas
2 jalapeño chiles, seeds removed, sliced
2 bay leaves
2 teaspoons salt
2 cups white wine vinegar

Fry the fish cubes in the oil until lightly browned. Remove and drain, reserving some oil. Sauté the onions, garlic, and carrots in the remaining oil until slightly soft.

Place the fish in a nonmetallic bowl and top with the onions, garlic, carrots, and the oil from the pan.

Combine the remaining ingredients and simmer for 10 minutes.

Pour the sauce over the fish and marinate for at least 2 days.

*Serves:* 6 to 8

*Serving Suggestions:* Serve either cold or at room temperature, in small dishes with toothpicks.

*Note:* This recipe requires advance preparation.

HEAT SCALE: 6

---

### What Chile Belters Do When They Run Out of Escabeche

"They would eat another kind of stew, of frogs, with green chile; they would eat a stew of those fish called *axolotl,** with yellow chile; they also ate kinds of tadpoles, and a stew of ants with *chiltecpitl.*"—from a pre-Conquest Mexican cookbook

*A South of the Border salamander—ED. NOTE.

# HAWAIIAN SHRIMP KABOBS

The hot and sweet taste of the basting sauce blends well with tropical fruits. Experiment with mangoes, papayas, and bananas.

1 tablespoon crushed red chile
2 teaspoons Picante Sauce (page 6)
2 teaspoons fresh ginger, peeled and grated
1 can (16 ounces) pineapple chunks, drained (reserve juice)
2 tablespoons soy sauce
1/4 cup sugar
1/3 cup vinegar
2 tablespoons cornstarch mixed with 1/4 cup water
1 pound medium shrimp, shelled and de-veined

Combine the chile, Picante Sauce, ginger, 1 cup reserved pineapple juice (additional juice may be needed to make 1 cup), soy sauce, sugar, and vinegar. Bring to a boil, reduce the heat, and simmer for 10 minutes.

Mix the cornstarch and water and slowly add the cornstarch mixture to the pineapple mixture, stirring constantly until thickened.

Alternate the shrimp and pineapple chunks on skewers. Dip each skewer in the sauce and then broil, turning frequently over charcoal or under the broiler until lightly browned, about 5 minutes.

*Yield:* 8 to 10 skewers
HEAT SCALE: 5

---

*Capsaicin Gastric Irritant? Medical Mystery Continues*

Chile peppers are commonly accused of causing heartburn and upset stomachs, yet in some cultures the pods are used as a *cure* for these very maladies. Now, what's the deal here? Dr. Arnold Levy, who is vice-president of the American Digestive Disease Society, states flatly: "Precious little data are available anywhere in any language on the effects of hot, spicy foods on the digestive tract."

# HOT CRAB CAPS

This unusual and elegant appetizer can also be served as a side dish with roasted meat.

6 tablespoons butter
1 tablespoon flour
½ cup light cream
¼ teaspoon salt
15 to 20 large mushrooms
5 green chiles, skinned, seeds removed, chopped
4 green onions, chopped fine (including greens)
6 ounces cooked crabmeat, chopped fine
1 tablespoon Cognac
¼ cup cracker crumbs

Melt 1 tablespoon of the butter in a heavy saucepan, add the flour, and cook 2 minutes, making sure the flour does not brown. Slowly stir in the cream, add the salt, and cook, stirring constantly until the sauce is thick. Remove from the heat and set aside.

Remove the stems from the mushrooms and chop them fine. Sauté the chopped stems, chile, and green onions in 2 tablespoons of the butter in a large skillet until soft. Stir in the crab and Cognac. Add the reserved sauce, mix well, and remove from the heat.

Melt 2 tablespoons of the butter in a baking pan. Brush the bottoms of the mushrooms caps with the butter and bake, stem sides down, for 5 minutes in a 350°F oven.

Melt the remaining butter and stir in the bread crumbs. Remove the mushroom caps from oven and turn them upside down. Mound the crab mixture in the mushroom caps. Top with the bread crumb mixture and return to the oven for an additional 15 minutes.

*Yield:* 15 to 20 caps
HEAT SCALE: 4

# PUNGENT PICKLED SALMON

This recipe makes Norway an honorary member of the Chile Belt.

10 pieces smoked salmon
1 tablespoon ground red chile
¾ cup vinegar
2 teaspoons sugar
¼ cup water
1 onion, thinly sliced and separated into rings

Soak the salmon in water for 4 hours, then drain.

Combine the chile, vinegar, sugar, and water and bring to a boil.

Layer the salmon and onions in a nonmetallic bowl and pour the chile mixture over the top. Marinate, covered, in the refrigerator, for 2 to 3 days. Drain before serving.

*Serves:* 8 to 10

*Serving Suggestions:* Arrange the salmon on a platter and garnish with the onion rings. The salmon may be cut into smaller pieces and served on crackers or toasted bread rounds.

*Note:* This recipe requires advance preparation.

HEAT SCALE: 3

---

*How Chile Peppers Conquered the World*
*Part II—European Addiction*

"Eating paprika is nothing but a habit, but one finds it agreeable. If there is time for it, plant some paprika in flower pots. . . . When it is ripe, they pick the pods, string them, then dry them on an oven and pound them. It is pungent, but only for a short time and makes the stomach feel very warm." —Count Hoffmannsegg, 1794

# MARINATED HOT SHRIMP

Because scampi are nearly impossible to find in the United States, we've substituted shrimp in this Mediterranean dish.

2 tablespoons crushed red chile
1 cup olive oil
1 tablespoon finely chopped fresh parsley
2 tablespoons garlic, minced
2 tablespoons chopped green onions (including greens)
¼ cup white wine
1 pound large shrimp, shelled and deveined
Chopped green onions or chives for garnish (optional)

Combine all ingredients except the shrimp in a nonmetallic bowl. Marinate the shrimp in the mixture for at least 8 hours or overnight in the refrigerator.

Bake the shrimp with the marinade in a shallow baking dish for 10 minutes in a 350°F oven, turning and basting with the marinade. Do not overcook or the shrimps may toughen.

*Yield:*   20 to 25 shrimp.

*Serving Suggestions:*   Serve hot, with the marinade in a chafing dish. Garnish with chives. Provide toothpicks for spearing the shrimp, and have a basket of Italian or French bread for dipping in the marinade.

*Note:*   This recipe requires advance preparation.

HEAT SCALE:   5

---

*List of Chile Belt Countries with Zero Chile Acreage*

| | |
|---|---|
| Bermuda | Monaco |
| Cyprus | Republic of Palau |
| Qatar | Somali Republic |

# SHARP COCONUT SHRIMP

The crunchy texture and pungent coconut taste make this Caribbean specialty a real treat.

3 tablespoons crushed red chile
½ cup flour
½ cup beer
1 pound large shrimp, shelled and deveined but with tails left on
½ cup fresh coconut meat, shredded, or
   ½ cup grated coconut
Vegetable oil for deep-fat frying

Combine the chile and flour slowly, adding the beer to make a batter. Dip each shrimp in the batter and then roll in the coconut.

Deep-fry the shrimp in 350°F oil until golden, then drain.

*Yield:* 20 to 25 shrimps.

*Serving Suggestion:* Serve arranged around a bowl of Hot and Sour Sauce (recipe follows).

HOT AND SOUR SAUCE
2 teaspoons Picante Sauce (page 6) or
   Tabasco
½ cup vinegar
2 tablespoons catsup
1 tablespoon soy sauce
½ cup sugar
2 tablespoons constarch mixed with 2 teaspoons water

Heat all the ingredients except the cornstarch mixture to boiling. Slowly stir in the cornstarch and heat until thickened.

*Yield:* ½ cup

HEAT SCALE: 5

# CLAMS CALIENTE

Interesting variations on this dish include substituting oysters or scallops for the clams and lemon juice for the clam juice.

2 cloves garlic, minced.
1 tablespoon minced green onions
1 tablespoon butter
1 to 2 tablespoons flour
2 cans (8 ounces each) minced clams,
    drained (reserve juice)
½ cup heavy cream
1 tablespoon Picante Sauce (page 6)
¼ cup grated Parmesan cheese
½ teaspoon Worcestershire sauce
1 teaspoon dried oregano
2 teaspoons finely chopped fresh cilantro
    (optional)
Vegetable oil for deep-fat frying

Sauté the garlic and green onions in the butter until soft. Add the flour and heat, stirring constantly. Make sure the flour does not brown.

Meanwhile, combine ¼ cup reserved clam juice and the cream. Slowly add this to the flour mixture, stirring constantly. Simmer over low heat until the sauce is very thick. Remove from the heat.

Add the remaining ingredients, except the oil, and refrigerate for at least 4 hours.

Using about a teaspoon of the mixture, form 1-inch balls. Deep fry the balls in 350°F oil for 1 to 2 minutes. Remove, drain, and keep warm.

*Yield:* 15 to 20

*Serving Suggestion:* Serve in a chafing dish with a mustard dip prepared from 2 tablespoons of Dijon-style mustard combined with ½ cup of sour cream.

*Note:* This recipe requires advance preparation. The clam balls can be refrigerated for 2 days. To reheat, place on a wire rack in a 425°F oven for 5 to 6 minutes. The clam balls can also be frozen. To reheat, thaw in the refrigerator and place on a wire rack in a 350°F oven for 10 minutes.

HEAT SCALE: 4

# PIQUANT POM-POM SHRIMP

A visually appealing appetizer—the noodles double the size of the shrimip.

2 teaspoons cayenne powder
2 teaspoons peeled and minced fresh ginger
2 tablespoons rice wine or dry sherry
1 pound large shrimp, shelled and deveined but with tails left on
2 tablespoons flour
1 egg, beaten
1 cup Chinese rice noodles, broken in half
Vegetable oil for deep-fat frying

Combine the cayenne, ginger, and rice wine in a nonmetallic bowl. Add the shrimp and marinate for at least 4 hours.

Dust the shrimp with the flour, dip into the egg, and roll in the noodles until coated.

Deep-fry in 350°F oil until golden and the noodles have puffed. Remove and drain.

*Yield:* 20 to 25

*Serving Suggestions:* Serve as is or with a dipping sauce such as Coconut Pepper Sauce (page 12) or Hot and Sour Sauce (page 66).

*Note:* This recipe requires advance preparation.

HEAT SCALE: 3

---

### No Wonder There Are So Many Brands of Prepared Mustard

According to food expert Waverley Root, mustard was a symbol of fecundity to the ancient Hindus. No wonder. He reveals that three quarters of a pound of black mustard seed or two pounds of white mustard seeds will produce a half-billion second-generation mustard seeds from *one acre* of land in a good year.

# CLAMS PICA-PICA

Vary the taste with oysters or mussels in place of the clams.

4 jalapeño chiles, seeds removed, chopped
1 large tomato, peeled and chopped
1 small onion, chopped fine
2 cloves garlic, chopped
1 tablespoon lime juice
12 clams in the shell
Chopped cilantro, parsley, or onion rings
    for garnish (optional)

Place the chiles, tomato, onion, garlic, and lime juice in a blender and puree until smooth.

Open the clams and discard the top shell, leaving the meat in the bottom shell. Place the clams in a shallow pan, meat side up. Place a small amount of sauce on each clam and bake in a 400°F oven for 15 minutes.

*Yield:* 12

*Serving Suggestion:* Place on a platter and garnish with chopped cilantro or parsley and raw onion rings.

*Variations:* Substitute oysters for the clams.

HEAT SCALE: 7

---

### The Neuron Bomb

Studies at the University of Basel in Switzerland have determined that capsaicin attacks type "B" neurons and deadens them after repeated contact. In some way the pungent chemical in chiles blocks pain sensations on the way to the brain. The brain registers the sensations as the heat we feel, and repeated usage lessens the sensation—hence the tolerance all chile heads experience.

# SPICY SALMON WON TONS

Keep a supply of these won tons in the freezer for quick hors d'ouvres when unexpected guests drop by.

*½ cup Cuernavaca Salsa (page 28)*
*1 can (6 ounces) salmon meat, drained*
*4 ounces cream cheese*
*2 cloves garlic, minced*
*2 tablespoons minced onion*
*⅓ cup crushed pineapple, drained*
*3 tablespoons bread crumbs*
*1 pound won ton skins*
*Vegetable oil for deep-fat frying*

Combine all the ingredients, except the won tons and oil, and thoroughly mix. Assemble and deep-fry as for the Wildest Won Tons (page 51).

*Yield:* 4 dozen
*Serving Suggestion:* Serve with Hot and Sour Sauce (page 66).
HEAT SCALE: 5

---

### *Only an Aggie Would Emasculate a Jalapeño*

Agronomists at Texas A&M have developed a completely nonpungent jalapeño pepper. The theory was that processors could then add capsaicin in measured amounts to assure that "mild" and "blistering" could be accurately determined. But the pepper has failed to generate a commercial market, perhaps because chile heads today prefer chance to regularity.

# GINGERED SHRIMP

The Oriental overtones of this spicy appetizer provide a perfect beginning for a Chinese feast.

4 green chiles, skinned, seeds removed, chopped
2 teaspoons peeled and minced fresh ginger
1 pound shrimp, shelled and deveined, chopped fine
1 teaspoon minced fresh chives
1 tablespoon minced fresh parsley
½ cup finely chopped water chestnuts
1 teaspoon soy sauce
½ teaspoon salt
½ teaspoon sugar
1 egg, beaten
2 tablespoons cornstarch
1 cup bread crumbs
Vegetable oil for deep-fat frying

Combine all the ingredients, except the bread crumbs and oil, and mix thoroughly.

Using about a teaspoon of the shrimp mixture each time, form 1-inch balls. Roll in bread crumbs. Deep-fry the balls in 350°F oil until golden brown. Remove and drain.

*Yield:* 20 to 25

*Serving Suggestions:* Serve in a chafing dish with toothpicks and a dipping sauce such as Curry-Pepper Dip (page 26) or Hefty Horseradish Sauce (page 29) on the side.

HEAT SCALE: 5

---

**What to Do with Guests Who Stay Too Long Nibbling on These Recipes**

"If the ripe pods of the *Capsicum* pepper are thrown into the fire, they will raise strong and noisome vapours, which occasion vehement sneezing and coughing and often vomiting, in those who are near the place, or in the room where they are burnt."—Philip Miller, *Gardener's Dictionary,* 1768

# 6 · Baked but Blazing

Empanaditas (facing page) are pungent Latin American pastry treats with close relatives in India (page 74) and Jamaica (page 76). By substituting phyllo dough, a new amalgam emerges: Chile-Cheese Tiropetas (page 78), which illustrates the Athens-Albuquerque connection.

Resembling Mount St. Helens in both form and fire, Peppery Puffs (page 79) explode when explored with fork and tongue.

Co-author Gerlach believes that baked foods taste better if served warm. She offers as evidence Scorching Sausage Biscuits (page 83), another breakfast alternative. They can combine with Carnitas Caliente (page 53) for a really blazing breakfast; they also make perfect appetizers.

And Baked but Blazing items blend well with Dangerous Dips to create new dimensions—and heat scale ratings—of fiery appetizers.

# EMPANADITAS

These are little empanadas, which are found in every Spanish-speaking area of the Americas.

2 cups flour
2 teaspoons baking powder
1/2 teaspoon salt
1/3 cup shortening
1/3 cup cold water
1 egg, beaten
Startling Indian Samosa Filling (page 74),
   Powerful Picadillo (page 75), or Jamaican Beef Patties (page 76), or use won ton fillings (pages 50 and 70).
Vegetable oil for deep-fat frying
   (optional)

Sift the dry ingredients together. With a pastry blender, cut in the shortening until the flour resembles fine crumbs. Add just enough of the water so that the mixture holds together. Chill for 1 hour.

Roll the dough out 1/8 inch thick and cut into circles 3 inches in diameter.

Place the filling on one half of each circle and fold over. Moisten the edges with water and crimp with a fork to seal.

Brush the top of each with egg and bake in a 400°F oven for 15 to 20 minutes or until golden brown. Or, the empanaditas can also be deep-fat-fried in 365° F oil until golden brown. Remove and drain.

Yield: 20 to 24 pastries

Note: Empanaditas can be frozen unbaked for 2 months, or if baked, 4 months. To reheat cooked empanaditas, thaw overnight in the refrigerator and bake in an 400°F oven for 15 minutes.

HEAT SCALE: Varies according to filling selected.

# STARTLING INDIAN SAMOSA FILLING

Makes curried empanaditas.

*1 tablespoon crushed red chile*
*2 tablespoons curry powder (Madras pre-*
 *ferred)*
*2 teaspoons ground ginger*
*1 pound ground beef or lamb*
*1 large onion, chopped fine*
*2 cloves garlic, chopped fine*
*1 tart apple, cored, peeled, finely chopped*

Sauté the beef until brown and crumbly. Add the remaining ingredients and sauté until the onion is soft. Pour off any excess fat, leaving enough to hold the mixture somewhat together.

*Yield:*  Enough for 20 to 24 pastries
*Serving Suggestion:*  Use to fill Empanaditas (page 73).

HEAT SCALE:  6

---

*That's Fine, but We Demand an Oscar Next*

"The *Capsicum* has the distinction of being one of the few plants, if not the only one, that played a leading role in winning a Nobel Prize. Scientific history has recorded that the discovery of vitamin C involved the pepper. The first pure vitamin C was produced in 1928 by the Hungarian Albert Szent-Gyorgyi, M.D., Ph.D., who was awarded the Nobel Prize for physiology and medicine in 1937." —Jean Andrews

# POWERFUL PICADILLO

A Cuban empanadita filling.

1 pound ground beef
5 jalapeño or serrano chiles, seeds removed, chopped fine
1 large onion, chopped fine
2 cloves garlic, chopped fine
⅓ cup Tunisian Pepper Sauce (page 10)
½ cup raisins
1 teaspoon ground cinnamon
¼ teaspoon ground cloves
½ cup chopped almonds

Sauté the beef until brown and crumbly. Add the chiles, onion, garlic, and continue to sauté until the onions are soft. Drain off any excess fat.

Add the remaining ingredients and thoroughly heat.

*Yield:* Enough for 20 to 24 pastries
*Serving Suggestion:* Use to fill Empanaditas (page 73).
HEAT SCALE: 6

---

### Peppers as Panacea, M–Z

Still more medical maladies treated with chiles. These are conditions reputed to be treated or cured by chile peppers, whether by diet or other application. Only those indicated with an asterisk have any medical basis.

Malaria, night blindness, rheumatism, seasickness, *scurvy, sore throats, stomach ache, tooth ache, tumors, wounds.

# JAMAICAN BEEF PATTIES

Often lamb or goat is substituted for beef in this classic Caribbean filling.

2 pounds ground beef, lamb, or goat
2 onions, minced
4 green onions, chopped fine (including greens)
3 jalapeño or serrano chiles, seeds removed, chopped fine
2 tablespoons cooking oil
2 cups bread crumbs
2 tablespoons curry powder
1 cup water
1 tablespoon salt
1 teaspoon dried thyme

Sauté the beef, onions, and chiles together in the oil. When the meat is just browned, add the bread crumbs, curry powder, water, salt, and thyme.

Cook over low heat for 30 minutes, then remove from heat, drain off any excess fat, and cool.

*Yield:* 20 to 24 patties

*Serving Suggestion:* Use to fill Empanaditas (page 73).

*Note:* If using for Empanaditas, add 1 tablespoon curry powder to the flour in the pastry for that recipe.

HEAT SCALE: 6

---

### Tam-o'-Shanter Cuisine

The hot chile most prevalent in Jamaican cooking is the "Scot's Bonnet," so named for its tam-o'-shanter shape and red and yellow coloration. It is actually a habanero, one of the hottest peppers in the world. Often they are cut into thin slivers and mixed with lime juice and salt as a condiment, and they are commonly preserved by canning in "pickles" with onions and sweet peppers for future use when fresh chiles may not be available.

# CHILE CHEESE TWISTS

Try these in place of pretzels at your next party.

1 cup flour
5 teaspoons crushed red chile
1/2 teaspoon ground ginger
1/2 teaspoon salt
1/3 cup butter
1 1/2 cups sharp grated Cheddar cheese
1 teaspoon Worcestershire sauce
4 to 5 tablespoons cold water
1 egg, beaten
2 tablespoons sesame seeds (optional)

Mix the flour, chile, ginger, and salt together. With a pastry blender, cut in the butter until the mixture resembles fine crumbs. Add the cheese and mix well.

Mix the Worcestershire sauce with 2 tablespoons of water, sprinkle over the flour mixture and mix lightly. Add more water until the mixture will hold together. Chill for 1 hour.

Roll the dough into a 1/4-inch-thick square on a floured board. Cut the dough into 1/2-inch strips 4 to 5 inches long.

Hold each strip at the ends and twist in opposite directions. Brush the dough with egg and top with the seeds. Place on a greased baking sheet and bake in a 350°F oven for 15 minutes, or until golden brown.

*Yield:* 40

*Note:* These twists can be made ahead of time and frozen. To serve, thaw overnight in the refrigerator and reheat in a warm oven.

HEAT SCALE: 8

# CHILE-CHEESE TIROPETAS

Phyllo pastry, also known as strudel dough, is one of the most versatile party pastries. Be sure never to let the dough dry out.

1/2 cup skinned, seeded, chopped green chiles
1 cup creamed cottage cheese
8 ounces feta cheese, finely crumbled
4 ounces cream cheese
3 eggs, slightly beaten
1/4 cup finely chopped fresh parsley
1/4 teaspoon ground black pepper
3/4 cup butter, melted
1/2 pound (20 sheets) phyllo pastry (see note)

Combine the chiles, cheeses, eggs, parsley, and pepper to make the filling

Brush a baking pan with butter and layer with half the Phyllo sheets, brushing with butter between each sheet. Spread the cheese mixture evenly over the sheets and top with the remaining sheets—each layer individually brushed with butter. You can keep the sheets from drying out during this process by covering them with a damp towel.

With a very sharp knife, cut the sheets into squares, triangles, diamonds, or rounds before baking.

Bake at 375°F for 40 minutes or until golden brown.

*Yield:* 40 to 50 (will vary according to size of cut).

*Note:* Phyllo pastry—paper thin sheets of flaky pastry that are brushed with butter between layers, filled, and baked—is similar to strudel. It can be purchased, frozen, in Greek specialty stores and some supermarkets.

This recipe can be made in advance and frozen after baking. Reheat on a rack in a 350°F oven before serving.

HEAT SCALE: 4

# PEPPERY PUFFS

These chile-cheese puffs provide welcome relief from commercial crackers.

⅓ cup skinned, seeded, chopped green
    chiles
¼ cup finely chopped onion
1 clove garlic, chopped fine
1 cup plus 1 tablespoon butter
2 cups flour
½ teaspoon salt
1 teaspoon hot dry mustard
½ cup sour cream
1 cup grated sharp Cheddar cheese

Sauté the chile, onion, and garlic in the 1 tablespoon butter until the onion is soft. Remove, drain, and cool. Combine the flour and salt, and with a pastry blender, cut in the 1 cup butter until crumbly.

Stir the mustard into the sour cream and add to the flour mixture. Combine until the mixture holds together.

Add the cheese, cover, and refrigerate for at least four hours or preferably overnight.

On a floured board, roll the pastry ¼ inch thick. Cut into circles or squares 1½ inches in diameter.

Bake on an ungreased baking sheet in a 375°F oven for 15 to 20 minutes, or until puffed and golden.

*Yield:*  4 to 5 dozen.

*Note:*  This recipe requires advance preparation.

HEAT SCALE:  4

---

*Authentic Native American Evidence of Pungency Addiction Syndrome (PAS)*

On the Papago Reservation in Arizona, the demand for the wild chile pepper, chiltepin, is so great that the tiny fruits are smuggled in from Mexico and sold for over $15 a pound.

# PIQUANT POTATO SKINS

This recipe adds the one ingredient missing in most restaurant versions of this dish—chile heat. Don't discard the potato meat—it can be made into another delicious hors d'oeuvre (see the recipe that follows).

6 large baking potatoes (Russet preferred)
1/3 cup butter, melted
1 cup chopped onion
10 green chiles, skinned, seeds removed, diced
3/4 cup each grated sharp Cheddar and Monterey Jack cheese

Bake the potatoes until soft to the touch and let cool.

Cut each potato into quarters and scoop out most of the potato, leaving a 1/4-inch-thick shell.

Brush the potato shells inside and out with butter and place on a baking sheet. Bake for 12 to 15 minutes in a 450°F oven until crisp. Remove from the oven.

Fill the shells with the onion and chopped chiles, top with the mixed cheeses, and place under the broiler until the cheese melts.

*Yield:* 24

HEAT SCALE: 5

---

### Duck Hunters and Hoboes Take Note

Since the capsaicin in chiles stimulates the blood circulation and warms us up, one sage has suggested sprinkling cayenne powder in your socks if you have a tendency toward cold feet. A similar apocryphal story holds that hoboes crossing the Rockies in boxcars would first steal a jar of pickled jalapeños for the trip to keep warm.

# LIGHTNING LATKES

Some powerfully pungent potato pancakes.

6 *green chiles, skinned, seeds removed, chopped fine*
2 *cups cooked potato meat (see facing recipe)*
2 *eggs*
2 *tablespoons flour*
*Vegetable oil for frying*

Combine all the ingredients except the oil in a blender and puree until smooth.

Fry 2 tablespoons of the potato mixture at a time in ¼ inch of hot oil until brown. Turn and brown the other side.

Remove from the oil and drain.

*Yield:*   30 to 40 potato pancakes
*Serving Suggestion:*   Serve warm with sour cream on top.
HEAT SCALE:   5

---

*Chile Belters! Now You Can Feed Your Addiction While on Vacation*

For seasoned travelers, the authors offer the following chile pepper translations:

French: *Piment enragé*
Italian: *Peperone*
Russian: *Struchkovy pyerets*

Japanese: *Togarashi*
Portuguese: *Pimentao picante*
Arabic: *Filfil*

# SCORCHING SAUSAGE BISCUITS

Although not a true biscuit because they don't rise, these are some of the simplest and fastest to prepare of the fiery finger foods.

4 teaspoons crushed red chile
1 cup flour
2 teaspoons baking powder
2 cups grated sharp Cheddar cheese
1 pound hot sausage, removed from casings

Combine all ingredients and shape into 1½-inch balls. Place on ungreased baking sheets. Bake in a 400°F oven for 25 minutes or until golden brown.

*Yield:* 4 to 5 dozen

*Note:* These can be prepared in advance and frozen. To reheat, thaw overnight in the refrigerator and reheat, on a rack, in a 350°F oven.

HEAT SCALE: 7

---

*How Chile Peppers Conquered the World*
*Part III—Slaver's Slabber Sauce*

Botanist S. A. McClure theorizes that chile peppers were probably introduced into Africa by slave ship captains who utilized them as food for their captives. And, according to historian Daniel Mannix, "slabber sauce," which consisted of palm oil, flour, water, and chiles, was poured over "horse beans" as the second meal of the day aboard slave ships.

# Index

Startling Shrimp Spread, 36
Steak, grilled, in fajitas, 49
Stuffed cucumbers, scorching, 5
Sunbelt Salsa, 7
Szent-Gyorgyi, Albert, 74

Tacos, rolled, 41
Tangy Chicken Tidbits, 55
Tea, as antidote to PAS, 35
Tiropetas, chile-cheese, 78
Tong, Michael, 27
Tunisian Pepper Sauce, 10

Vegetables
  cucumbers
    sliced, caliente, 14
    stuffed, scorching, 5

mushroom caps, capsicum, 9
papper rings, pungent, 16
pickled power, 13

Wildest Won Tons, the, 50
Wild Guacamole, 18
Won tons
  spicy salmon, 70
  the wildest, 50

Yakitori, 58
Yogurt, as antidote to PAS, 25

Zesty Skewered Chicken, 58

## The Crossing Press

publishes a full selection of cookbooks.
To receive our current catalog,
please call, toll-free
1-800-777-1048.